AF605153

TASMANIA

First published in 2025 by New Holland Publishers
Sydney, Australia.
newhollandpublishers.com

 A record of this book is held at the National Library of Australia.

ISBN : 9781760797812

Managing Director: Fiona Schultz
General Manager/Publisher: Olga Dementiev
Designer: Andrew Davies
Production Director: Arlene Gippert
Printed in China

TASMANIA

THE GULF WAR
AFGHANISTAN
IRAQ

JAMS.

A.G. OGILVIE K.C.
PREMIER
1934–39

MURRAY ST
KEEP
LEFT

25

TASMANIA

- Tasmania is the only Australian state that is an island. It is the **26th** largest island in the world.
- The nick name for Tasmania is '**The Apple Isle**'.
- The highest mountain is **Mount Ossa** located in the heart of Cradle Mountain where you'll find some of the most ancient and tallest trees in the world.
- It takes just **two and a half hours** to drive from Hobart (south) to Launceston (north).
- Out of the eleven UNESCO World Heritage listed convict sites in Australia, **five** are found in Tasmania.
- Tasmania has several mammals found nowhere else in the world, such as the **Tasmanian Devil**.
- **Cascade Brewery** was established in 1824 and is still operating today.
- Tasmania is known for its **fresh produce** from honey to cherries, but it also grows black truffles and has the best lobster and wild abalone in Australia.
- Tasmania has the **cleanest air** in the world.